SWEDEN

in pictures

Prepared by Jo McDonald

**VISUAL
GEOGRAPHY
SERIES**

STERLING
PUBLISHING CO., INC. NEW YORK

Oak Tree Press Co., Ltd.
London & Sydney

VISUAL GEOGRAPHY SERIES

Afghanistan
Alaska
Argentina
Australia
Austria
Belgium and Luxembourg
Berlin—East and West
Bolivia
Brazil
Bulgaria
Canada
The Caribbean (English-Speaking Islands)
Ceylon (Sri Lanka)
Chile
China
Colombia
Costa Rica
Cuba
Czechoslovakia
Denmark

Dominican Republic
Ecuador
Egypt
El Salvador
England
Ethiopia
Fiji
Finland
France
French Guiana
Ghana
Greece
Greenland
Guatemala
Guyana
Haiti
Hawaii
Holland
Honduras
Hong Kong
Hungary

Iceland
India
Indonesia
Iran
Iraq
Ireland
Islands of the Mediterranean
Israel
Italy
Ivory Coast
Jamaica
Japan
Jordan
Kenya
Korea
Kuwait
Lebanon
Liberia
Madagascar (Malagasy)
Malawi

Malaysia and Singapore
Mexico
Morocco
Nepal
New Zealand
Nicaragua
Nigeria
Norway
Pakistan and Bangladesh
Panama and the Canal Zone
Paraguay
Peru
The Philippines
Poland
Portugal
Puerto Rico
Rhodesia
Rumania
Russia
Saudi Arabia

Scotland
Senegal
South Africa
Spain
The Sudan
Surinam
Sweden
Switzerland
Tahiti and the French Islands of the Pacific
Taiwan
Tanzania
Thailand
Tunisia
Turkey
Uruguay
The U.S.A.
Venezuela
Wales
West Germany
Yugoslavia

Jenny Lind, known as the "Swedish Nightingale," was one of the greatest coloratura sopranos of all time. The remarkable range and quality of her voice thrilled people all over the world in the mid-1800's.

ACKNOWLEDGMENTS

The publishers wish to thank the following for the use of the photographs in this book: Scandinavian Airlines System; Scandinavia House, New York; The American Swedish News Exchange, New York.

The publishers wish to thank Mr. Allan Kastrup and Mr. Sigfrid Leijonhufvud of the Swedish Information Service, New York, and especially thank Mr. Kenneth Dutfield, Stockholm, for checking the authenticity of the information in this book.

Winter lake fishing in the high provinces is cold but exciting.

CONTENTS

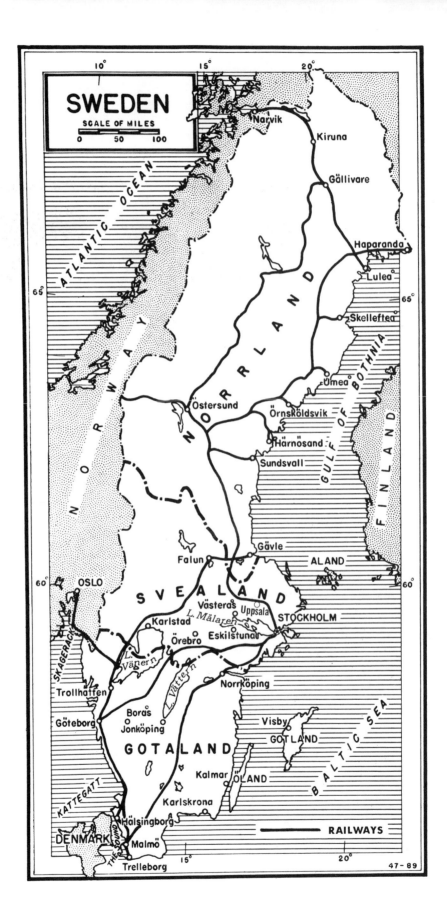

SWEDEN

SCALE OF MILES

0   50   100

ATLANTIC OCEAN

Narvik
Kiruna
Gällivare
Haparanda
Luleå
Skellefteå
Umeå
Östersund
Örnsköldsvik
Härnösand
Sundsvall

N O R R L A N D

N O R W A Y

GULF OF BOTHNIA

FINLAND

Falun
Gävle
ALAND

S V E A L A N D

OSLO
Västerås   Uppsala
Karlstad   L. Mälaren
Örebro   Eskilstuna   STOCKHOLM

SKAGERAC

L. Vänern

L. Vättern

Norrköping

Trollhätten

Borås
Jonköping
Göteborg

Visby
GOTLAND

G O T A L A N D

BALTIC SEA

Kalmar   ÖLAND

KATTEGATT

Karlskrona

Hälsingborg

DENMARK   Malmö

Trelleborg

RAILWAYS

47-89

The Vikings left rune stones like this one in Ostergötland wherever they went. They usually bore terse statements like: "Erik the good conquered his rival Olav Bloodyaxe here and cut down 160 men." Runes are the earliest surviving Swedish writing, dating back to about A.D. 800.

I. HISTORY

ABOUT 12,000 B.C. the land that is now Sweden began to emerge from the retreating icecap, and tribes of hunters and fishermen started moving in from the south. The fossil remains of these people indicate that they were of the same Nordic type as modern Scandinavians.

Sometime around 1500 B.C., a native skill at metal handicrafts developed. The beautiful urns, ornaments and weapons which have been found show that the art of working in bronze nearly equalled that of Greece. Such archaeological finds are increasingly filling the great gulfs of unknown history of these early times.

In Roman times the Götar (thought to be a branch of the Goths) inhabited the south of Sweden. In the 5th century A.D., the Goths took part in the great migrations as far south as the Black Sea, coming into contact with the Byzantine and Roman world. Goths returning

to the Baltic brought writing with them. Uppsala, now known as Old Uppsala and a village near modern Uppsala, became the capital of Sweden's other leading tribe, the Svear. A few centuries later, the Uppsala kings ruled both the Götar and the Svear, uniting the country under one crown.

THE VIKING ERA

Soon after A.D. 800, Norsemen became seafarers on a world scale. Each spring, these Vikings (which loosely meant "sea warriors") set out in their long narrow ships, powered by oars and a single square sail, on long expeditions to exchange goods, but killing and plundering if they met with resistance.

The Vikings of Denmark and southwestern Sweden directed their voyages towards Europe, the Norwegian Vikings crossed the Atlantic to

A relic of prehistoric Sweden, this stone tomb, "Hagerdösen," is 5,000 years old. It is on the Isle of Orust north of Göteborg.

Iceland, Greenland, and finally to America, while most of the Swedish Vikings sailed eastward across the Baltic Sea to Russia, whose very name, from *Rus*, applied to Swedes from the Baltic Coast, is supposed to date from the first régime the Vikings set up under their chieftain Rurik.

The ultimate aim of every young Viking voyager was to be a "berserk," that is, to fight without a shirt of mail or a shield, hurling himself into the fray with only a sword as a weapon. Most of our knowledge of these invaders comes from the lands they pillaged so ruthlessly for almost 200 years, since there are few actual Viking records. Consequently, their image has always been one of a brutal, uncivilized people, but in recent years more and more evidence has been unearthed revealing that the Norsemen did indeed have a developed culture, though one vastly different from its contemporaries in other parts of Europe. Their contribution to military and governmental concepts was considerable.

St. Olav, the patron saint of Norway and the subject of church murals all over Scandinavia, was a particularly bloodthirsty warrior. Olav the Big, as he was called, ruled from 1015 to 1030 and converted his subjects to Christianity by the sheer power of the axe. A battle he fought with his own rebellious subjects ended with his being axed himself (as in the painting). There was a total eclipse of the sun at the time, "proving" that Olav's deity was angry. Compared with the misrule of his successor, the reign of Olav rendered him eligible for sainthood in 1164.

The Abbey Church at Värnhem, completed in 1250 and recently restored, contains the tombs of 12th- and 13th-century kings.

MIDDLE AGES

During the Viking Age of the 9th and 10th centuries, Christian missionaries under St. Ansgar visited Sweden, but it was not until the end of the 11th century, when the magnificent, gold-hung temple of the Norse gods at Uppsala was levelled to the ground, that Christianity was really accepted. Small Christian churches began to dot the countryside. One of the most famous of Sweden's older temples is the beautiful Abbey Church that Saint Bridget built at Vadstena in the 14th century.

The Hanseatic League, a medieval association of trading towns based mainly in Germany, had by this time extended into Scandinavia. Visby in Gotland was a major city of the League. There were ceremonies, some of them sadistic, for merchants joining the League, and their power in imposing trade monopolies was often absolute.

When the weak King Erik died in 1250, his brother-in-law, the remarkable Birger Jarl, took over control of Sweden, ruling in the name of his son until his death in 1266. He created excellent domestic laws with peace as the keynote: "family peace," "church peace," and "peace in the government." Birger Jarl, the founder of Stockholm, was able to deal decisively with the Hanseatic League, then running rampant over Scandinavia. Instead of letting the League wreck Sweden's economy as it had Norway's, he was able to trade with it, finally establishing a strong central government. Birger Jarl's influence is felt to this day.

The idea of a united Scandinavia gave birth to the Union of Kalmar in 1397 when Denmark, Norway and Sweden agreed to unite. However, the Union was uneasy; power struggles and nationalism nourished by efforts to establish an absolute monarchy, always threatened to upset it. Sweden, fearing Denmark's domination, rebelled and wars followed, although the union between Denmark and Norway lasted until 1814.

7

Gustavus Adolphus, born in 1594, became king in 1611 and led a tremendous political and military expansion until his death in 1632. He had great personal influence, due in large part to his good education, his strong character and the exceptional assistance of his chancellor of state, Count Axel Oxenstjerna.

Another remarkable man in early Swedish history, mine-owner Engelbrekt Engelbrektsson, led a popular revolt against the Danish Union in 1435. This resulted in the representation of farmers and burghers in parliament, showing that the feudal system had not taken a firm hold in Sweden.

Many obstacles had to be met before national freedom was achieved. Attacks by the Danes penetrated to the very walls of Stockholm in 1471, and in 1520 Christian II of Denmark occupied that capital. That same year, 80 leading noblemen were massacred in the central square, a tragedy known as the "Stockholm Blood Bath."

NATIONAL LIBERTY

Out of this revolt a young nobleman, whose father had been one of the 80 beheaded, emerged to lead a peasant rebellion. Gustavus Vasa, called the "Builder of the Swedish Realm" because he laid the foundations of modern Sweden, drove the Danes out of Sweden in two years. He was elected king in 1523 and began one of the greatest eras in Swedish history. With the Protestant Reformation sweeping Europe, he established a Lutheran state church and placed mining, agriculture and commerce on a sound footing. Gustavus and his three sons, who one after the other succeeded him, were all great builders.

The powerful regent, Birger Jarl, first fortified Stockholm against raiding pirates in 1252, locking off the entrance to Lake Mälaren.

Christina was recognized as queen in 1632, when she was still a minor. Count Axel Oxenstjerna undertook the regency and it was not until 1644 that Christina came of age. Ten years later she abdicated, became a Catholic, and took up residence in Rome, where she died in 1689.

Gustavus Adolphus's daughter, Christina, succeeded her father when she came of age in 1644, and became a zealous, if unpopular, monarch. Seriously interested in the arts and learning, she granted moneys and lands lavishly to artists and scholars whom she liked. In 1654, having been secretly converted to Catholicism, she abdicated and left the country, settling in Rome. She left financial disorder behind her.

On the Swedish throne Christina was succeeded by her cousin, Charles X, who became another great warrior king. Under him Sweden acquired its natural boundaries to the south and southwest, at the expense of Denmark. In 1660, Charles X was succeeded by his son, Charles XI, who devoted himself primarily to administration and finance.

For 80 years Sweden was a great power, but new wars followed under the gallant young monarch Charles XII, and Sweden's star began to set. The king, like Hitler and Napo-

GUSTAVUS ADOLPHUS

Gustavus Adolphus, coming to the throne in 1611 at the age of 17, is sometimes called the "Northern Hurricane." Inheriting from his father three wars—against Denmark, Russia and Poland—he finally concluded them all with treaties. In 1630, his big moment came. The Hapsburg Empire, supporting the Roman Catholic cause, was in deadly conflict with the German Protestants. Fearing that the Hapsburgs might threaten Sweden after their invasion of Denmark, Gustavus Adolphus took the offensive with 16,000 men to rescue Protestantism. He made a victorious march through Leipzig, Nuremberg, Munich and Augsburg. In 1632, his army also won the terrible battle at Lutzen against the imperial army, but the king himself was killed. Gustavus Adolphus has remained, to this day, the Swedes' most highly regarded monarch.

The young Gustavus Eriksson, who became the great King Gustavus I Vasa, rallied the peasants of Dalarna (Dalecarlia) in 1520. One province after another came to his support, and he eventually won all of Sweden back from Denmark. He is therefore known as the founder of modern Sweden.

9

Drottningholm Palace, near Stockholm, had this charming theatre attached to it in 1764–66. It was the scene of much gaiety during the reign of Gustavus III, who himself wrote verse dramas for it and sometimes acted in them. The theatre is still used, as are the original costumes and stage sets. The wings were painted in 1784 by Jacob Mörck.

leon, made the fatal mistake of invading the heart of Russia and in 1709, he was badly defeated in the Battle of Poltava. Charles himself, wounded, escaped to Turkey. Returning to Sweden to fight Denmark with a new army, he was killed, while attacking the Norwegian fortress of Fredrikssten.

Although the Swedish dream of empire was over, a bloodless revolution had vested parliament with greater powers. The country, exhausted by war, found its new leader in Count Arvid Horn. Under his administration, 18th-century Sweden had a quick economic and spiritual recovery which led to a cultural renaissance in natural sciences and literature. Linnaeus, the father of botany, Celsius, who perfected the centigrade thermometer, and Swedenborg, the scientist and mystic, were three of the outstanding men who emerged.

On this wave of the fine arts, Gustavus III ascended the throne in 1771 and became Sweden's most courtly monarch, the "Actor King." He formed the Swedish Academy in imitation of the French, and developed the beautiful Drottningholm Court Theatre for staging plays and operas, but above all, he dreamed of raising Sweden again to a great power. The Russians, he thought, were threatening Finland and hoping to conquer Sweden. When Gustavus had won a great naval battle in 1790, they were forced to sign a peace without territorial change. Two years later, the king was assassinated by some disgruntled officers at a costume ball at the Opera House.

In 1809, Finland, long part of the Swedish realm and closely tied to Sweden politically, culturally, economically and linguistically, was

Jean Baptiste Bernadotte, as King Charles XIV John, founded the present dynasty. A brilliant general in the French Revolution and later one of Napoleon's marshals, Bernadotte was chosen by the Swedish government to succeed the old and childless Charles XIII. This equestrian statue of Charles XIV is one of the popular sights of Stockholm. ⟵

lost to Russia. The shock to the country was deep. Yet soon after this darkest hour a brilliant new figure appeared.

THE BERNADOTTE ASCENSION

The new leader was Jean Baptiste Bernadotte, who had been one of Napoleon's marshals and was to become the first of the present line of kings. His ascension to the throne came about by the merest fluke.

Gustavus IV Adolphus, the obstinate and unbalanced son of Gustavus III, had a venomous hatred of Napoleon and sided with England against him. After the loss of Finland to Russia, Sweden was in a desperate situation.

The Danes seemed ready to attack from the south and the west, while the Russians were preparing to pounce from the north. In Sweden's anguish, a revolution was raised to

The 14th-century cathedral at Lund boasts this beautiful astronomical clock with jousting knights on top, the four rulers of the winds and the signs of the zodiac. When the clock plays at noon the carved horsemen go into action. Lund is also famous for its open-air museum showing how people have lived since Viking times. ⟶

get rid of the monarch, and Colonel Aldersparre marched on Stockholm to arrest him. The king tried to escape and was actually chased throughout the palace before being caught and imprisoned in one of his summer castles.

The aged and childless Charles XIII was temporarily put on the throne while Sweden looked for a new king to found another dynasty. The first choice was Christian August, a Danish prince, who had dreams of restoring the old union of Scandinavia, but shortly after his arrival in Sweden he fell off his horse and died. Many Swedes suspected that Count Hans Axel Fersen, who had gallantly tried to rescue Marie Antoinette from the French guillotine, had caused the "accident." He was unjustly accused and dragged from his carriage by a drunken mob and killed in broad daylight—one of the saddest deeds in Sweden's history.

Skåne or Scania, which gives its name to Scandinavia, is the "Château Country." One of the most exciting of the medieval castles to be seen is Vittskövle, a private fortified stronghold with a moat, watchtower and drawbridge.

The country, obviously sick, needed new blood. Marshal Jean Bernadotte, who had been made Prince of Ponte Corvo by Napoleon, had led the French troops against Denmark and thus became known in Sweden. An enthusiastic lieutenant, Karl Mörner, was so convinced that only Bernadotte could restore the Swedish nation that he rushed to Paris and offered the crown to the former sergeant from Pau. Bernadotte, believing Mörner was Sweden's official emissary, accepted, and Mörner rushed back to give the good news to an astonished parliament. The Swedes had found a new candidate—one whom, so they believed, Napoleon himself was backing.

This misunderstanding pursued its fateful course when Bernadotte sent a French agent to the Swedish court to drop a loaded hint that France would help the destitute Swedes financially. A last-minute decision was made, when indeed Sweden's destiny hung by a thread, and Bernadotte became the real leader of Sweden in the autumn of 1810, when he was adopted by Charles XIII as heir apparent.

Thus began Sweden's present dynasty. Bernadotte soon proved to be an astute and successful ruler. Siding with Napoleon's enemies, he led an army against the Danes, forcing Denmark to cede Norway to Sweden. When the Norwegians balked, Charles John, as Bernadotte was now called, marched his soldiers to the border and forced Norway to capitulate. Norway united with Sweden under one king in a union which lasted until 1905, when it was peaceably dissolved.

In 1818, after the Congress of Vienna which ended the Napoleonic era, Bernadotte was crowned Charles XIV. From this time until the present, Sweden has not gone to war.

MODERN SWEDEN

By the middle of the 19th century, Sweden was again rocked within its borders, this time by the spread of poverty. The old farming economy had slumped and it was a time of general despair and intellectual decline. Large groups of people began leaving for America; yet new forces were at work in Sweden, and the delayed industrial revolution started. Steam-driven sawmills, expanding trade, increased urbanization and better transportation all helped to transform the country. Electoral reforms, the emergence of unions and a redefinition by the Swedes of their rôle in the world were all signs of Sweden's modernization.

August Strindberg, the prolific writer, novelist and playwright, was one of the prime movers in this era. He reacted fiercely against all forms of national complacency and put the people rather than their rulers on the stage. While the country's modernization was not quick enough to stop the drain of Sweden's population to America, the country entered into a period of growing prosperity.

Ever since the mid-1800's, Sweden has been growing more liberal in government and stronger in industrial development. After freedom of the press had been achieved, internal free trade and enfranchisement of the middle class followed. In the early 1900's, the Social Democratic party began its rise, later to become the predominant political entity in Sweden.

Under Gustavus V, king from 1907 until 1950, Sweden's liberalizing and development were continued, and social reforms of a new type began. Universal suffrage for men was introduced in 1909, and in 1913 the long process of welfare legislation began with old-age pension laws. At the same time, the Swedes became more determined to make neutrality the basis of their foreign policy. Sweden did not fight in either World War I or World War II, and is striving at the present time to ensure survival in case of a new war. It has not joined the North Atlantic Treaty Organization, although it is a member of the United Nations and many other international bodies.

Drottningholm, built in 1662–81 in the French style, is open to the public when the Royal Family is not in residence. The interior decor is especially fine, and the impressive park attracts many strollers.

Saint Bridget (14th century), one of the most remarkable women in Swedish history, like Joan of Arc heard "voices" which told her to found an order at Vadstena. First married to a nobleman, she bore eight children and served as Mistress of the Robes at court. On her husband's death she went to Rome and spent 23 years getting permission from the Pope to found the Order of Bridgetines. She returned to Vadstena to start building her abbey. When she died it was completed by her daughter Catherine, who was also canonized.

NEUTRALITY—FOR AND AGAINST

Joseph Stalin once said, speaking of Russia's foreign policy, "Gentlemen, we can do nothing about geography."

Sweden, an almost insular country late to become industrialized and therefore able to profit somewhat from other countries' mistakes, never felt particularly close to the European family of nations or wished to be drawn into the European movement.

A second factor in Sweden's decision to remain neutral is that, since 1814, Swedes have been living in peace and have become accustomed to thinking in peaceful terms.

A third factor is that Sweden has never been a colonial power. It sold its only colony—the little island of Saint Barthélemy in the West Indies—to France in 1877.

To understand Sweden's neutrality and non-participation in NATO, one must realize that Sweden is not ideologically neutral, but "neutral on the side of NATO." As with other neutral European powers, Austria and Switzerland, the theory is held that the country will resist invasion from the West and East alike, though if such invasions were simultaneous, the Swedes could scarcely hope to put up an effective resistance.

While it is never actually officially stated, the Swedes are well aware that the only real threat is from the East and that in the event of a third

Dalby, near Lund, has an 11th-century stone church, said to be the oldest in Skåne. It has a famous pillared west hall and this splendid crypt. Dalby was a see when Scandinavia first became Christianized.

Malmö, Sweden's third largest city and most southerly port, is only a ferry ride away from Copenhagen in Denmark. The Town Hall, built in 1546, when the city was still Danish, faces the statue of Charles X. Behind is St. Peter's Church.

world war, staunchly democratic Sweden would unquestionably find itself on the side of NATO. Strongly armed, with compulsory military service for every man between 18 and 47, Sweden nevertheless regards an isolated attack as unlikely.

Finland's relative freedom from Russian interference is generally attributed to Sweden's neutrality as well as Finland's. Finland is the only eastern European country without a communist-controlled government sharing a frontier with Russia, except for a small Norwegian frontier in the extreme north. Acting as a buffer between Sweden and the Soviet Union, Finland undoubtedly has Sweden's neutrality to thank for its own state of freedom.

What would Swedish policy be if the Russians took Finland? If this happened in peacetime, there is little doubt that Sweden would join NATO. However, Sweden maintains an almost unshakeable belief that Russia respects and appreciates its neutrality and because of this leaves Finland in peace.

Nonetheless, Sweden's neutral state is sup-

ported by substantial military strength. The Swedish air force is the fifth largest in the world. Defence expenditure is 5 per cent of the national income—more than in any of the minor NATO countries. There is no perceptible opposition to this among the general public except from members of the impotent, though vocal, Swedish Communist party, which represents less than 4 per cent of the electorate.

Engelbrekt Engelbrektsson, the mine-owner, led a peasant revolt in the mining district of Bergslagen in 1434. The meeting at Arboga in 1435 when Engelbrekt summoned the Four Estates (nobles, priests, burghers and peasants) is considered the first Swedish Riksdag or parliament. The statue is by Carl Milles.

It has been said that men and nations will only come to the defence of their closest "interests." If Finland is Sweden's closest interest, that is where neutrality might be pricked. Until then, Sweden is determined not to let the country be drawn into any major conflict.

At the same time that Sweden is steering a neutral course, it is preoccupied with the thought of war and has taken extensive precautions in the event of a national emergency. Insisting it is doing the only realistic thing, Sweden has built thousands of installations, both military and civilian, deep underground, and is prepared to evacuate nearly 3,000,000 citizens from towns and cities. There are underground shelters to accommodate about the same number of people. Along the Baltic, caves are hollowed out to such a high degree that warships can sail in and out.

Evacuation exercises are held at intervals, in which participation is entirely voluntary. Stockpiles of food, petroleum and industrial raw materials are stored underground in various parts of the country. In Stockholm, the large shelters beneath the city, which are now used as garages and warehouses, are capable of holding most of the city's population. The purpose of all this, of course, is to provide the best possible protection in the event of nuclear warfare.

This room in Övedskloster Castle is predominantly French in its interior decoration, but the fine china stove on the left is Germanic.

The origins of Stockholm are unknown. One Viking saga says that Agne, a warrior king, went off on a raid to Finland where he killed a chieftain and captured his daughter. On his way home he stopped on an island to drink the health of his new bride. Mead flowed freely. Agne fell asleep, and his bride freed her fellow Finnish prisoners, who promptly hanged Agne before sailing home. The shore where they stopped was called Agne Strand and is now part of Old Stockholm.

2. THE LAND

THE KINGDOM OF SVERIGE occupies nearly 175,000 square miles of the Scandinavian peninsula. Most of the larger rivers of this elongated country flow southeast from the mountainous spine through dense forests of spruce and fir and empty into the Gulf of Bothnia.

Sweden is divided geographically into three regions. Götaland in the south has its shores washed by the warm waters of the Gulf Stream and includes some of the chief ports of Sweden; Svealand, just north of the largest lakes, is called "central" Sweden although it is really within the bottom half of the country. Here Stockholm is located. Norrland covers well over half of Sweden, including mountainous Lapland, and borders on Norway, Finland and the Gulf of Bothnia. Sweden thus presents a wide variety of landscape: the fertile plains of the south, the wooded lake country, the seven-league forests of the north, and, finally, the barren slopes of the Arctic area.

17

The wooden churches found in the villages of north Sweden are often like square pavilions gaily painted in red and white.

This manor house in Södermanland, with its Maypole in the middle of the yard, is characteristic of central Sweden: a white, two-storied main building with a curb roof.

Stockholm's City Hall, St. Clara's Church spire, and the skyscrapers of the Hötorget shopping centre are silhouetted against the darkened sky.

In the gardens of Stockholm's splendid City Hall the figure "Dance" is laden with snow. Beyond is the waterway leading to Lake Mälaren.

Gripsholm Castle on Lake Mälaren is a three-hour steamer trip from Stockholm. Begun in the 1300's and rebuilt by Gustavus Vasa in 1535, Gripsholm houses a remarkable picture gallery, including the portrait that the sad King Erik XIV sent to Queen Elizabeth of England after his second proposal to her. Upon his dethronement he was held captive in the prison tower. Gustavus III, the "Actor King," built the little theatre attached to the castle. The courtyard is celebrated for its rune stones and the bronze cannon taken centuries ago in the Russian wars.

Iron, wood and water—these three words sum up Sweden's natural wealth. The great rivers, winding down through the massive forests, are harnessed to power stations to supply industry with its greatest resource, cheap electricity.

Since Götaland, Svealand and Norrland are very different in character, we will take them in turn, beginning with Svealand, the cradle of the country.

SVEALAND

Lying between Norrland and Götaland are the heartlands of Sweden. One of the oldest known important settlements is Uppsala, the university town north of Stockholm. Uppsala has witnessed 1,500 years of history, first as a religious capital of the Norsemen, as a political capital, as a Christian see, and then as an educational stronghold. One thousand years have passed since the Vikings made their last sacrifices to Thor, Odin, and Freya, the gods of war, wisdom and domesticity, in a temple hung with gold, and while Uppsala is now the seat of the Lutheran Archbishop of Sweden and of Uppsala University, the political power of the country has moved to Stockholm.

The city of Stockholm, placed on the waters, faces two directions, eastward across the islands of its archipelago to the Baltic Sea and westward over the fresh-water reaches of Lake Mälaren. Where the two meet, sea and lake, is Sweden's capital, "the knot of many waters." It was founded on an island about 1250 by Birger Jarl as a "padlock" to keep the Estonian pirates across the Baltic from raiding Lake Mälaren. The two expressions, "knot of many waters," and "padlock," describe Stockholm's physical appearance and stragetic site. Here the king in his island palace can watch almost every ship that docks nearby. Stockholm, with a population of about 800,000 and another 700,000 in the suburbs, is justly called "Queen of the Waters."

Svealand, with Stockholm guarding the eastern gateway, includes most of the central Lake District. Many of the 100,000 lakes in the country are here, wholly or in part. The three largest are Lake Mälaren, Lake Vättern and Lake Vänern, the third largest lake in Europe.

The picturesque Göta Canal is a 250-mile network of lakes, rivers and canals across the country from Stockholm to Göteborg. It was proposed in 1516 by Bishop Brask, principally to avoid paying the toll that Denmark levied on all shipping passing through the narrow straits between Malmö and Copenhagen. What is now southern Sweden was then part of Denmark and the powerful Danes had complete control of the straits. It was not until 1832, however, that the Göta Canal was completed. Today it is a popular tourist route.

Göteborg (Gothenburg), Sweden's gateway to the West, is a bustling port at the mouth of the Göta River on the Kattegat, the strait leading by way of the North Sea to the Atlantic. Founded in 1619 by Gustavus Adolphus, Göteborg has a population of about 425,000 and a big shipbuilding industry. At that time, the mouth of the Göta River, closely bounded by Norway on one side and Denmark on the other, was Sweden's only outlet to the Atlantic. This precious corridor the king protected still further with a deep moat and a broad canal. A statue of Gustavus Adolphus stands in Göteborg central square as though he still surveyed his handiwork with pride.

Included in discussions of central Sweden is Gotland, an island in the Baltic Sea. Visby, the walled capital of the island, with a history of 40 centuries, is a "city of ruins and roses." Its

Stockholm's white marble Royal Dramatic Theatre houses the top plays. Theatre, opera and ballet are all subsidized by the State, and touring companies carry "Hamlet" and other productions even to the Lapps in the North.

21

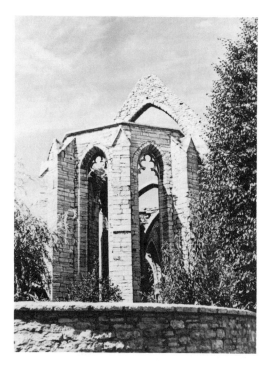

Now a popular resort with a modern port and manufacturing area, Visby is significant mainly for its history. As long ago as the 11th century, it was an important trading port of the Hanseatic League. From 1280 until the 19th century Visby was on the decline, and for many years it was owned by Denmark.

Modern apartment buildings in Stockholm are surrounded with trees wherever possible. Trees, flowers, water and, above all, the sun, gladden the Swedish heart. Many new housing blocks find ways to include them all. ⟶

Karlskrona, a Baltic port and the home of the Swedish Navy for nearly 300 years, has always been a sailor's town. The relief sculpture of Noah on his ark, welcoming the dove, adorns the local post office.

The Concert House steps in the Hötorget Market Square provide a handy meeting place for Stockholm residents. "Orpheus," Carl Milles' famous fountain group, is on the right.

Göteborg, Sweden's main port and second largest city, has a unique monument to the seamen lost in the First World War. On a pillar beside the Nautical Museum, "The Sailor's Wife," with her skirts blowing in the wind, looks out to sea for the returning ships.

Lund, primarily a university town, was founded nearly 1,000 years ago by King Canute, the Dane who conquered England and Scotland and also ruled most of Scandinavia. The University of Lund has an enrolment of about 7,000.

golden ages were from the 11th to the 14th centuries, during which it was the hub of trade with Russia, Constantinople and the Byzantine Empire.

North of Sweden's great lakes Vättern and Vänern lie the areas of Värmland and Dalarna. Dalarna, where many of the inhabitants still wear traditional costume and fiddlers play music for the Maypole dancers on Midsummer Day, is considered Sweden's most idyllic region. The word *Dalarna* means valleys—the lake and river valleys in the evergreen fir forests.

Falun, the name of both a city and a copper mine, is the heart of Dalarna. Here the oldest company in the world, Stora Kopparbergs Bergslags Aktiebolag, has been in business mining the ore since at least the 13th century, and the riches of the copper mine have financed many imperial adventures over the last 700 years. Falun's ore is also used in producing the characteristic red paint which covers so many Swedish farmhouses.

GÖTALAND

Götaland, the second large region of Sweden, includes the historic provinces of Skåne and Småland, at the extreme southern tip of the peninsula. There is an old tradition that while the Lord was busy making Skåne, the southern tip of Sweden, into a beautiful garden, the devil sneaked past him and made Småland a harsh, unyielding stretch of country. When the Lord saw what the devil had done, he said philosophically, "Oh, well, it's too late now to change Småland. I'll have to make people to go with it!" A man of Småland, the saying goes, can be put down on a stone island with only an axe in his hand and will turn it into a garden.

Skåne, close to Denmark, *is* really a garden and was for centuries part of the Danish realm.

Not until 1658, when Charles X threatened to attack Copenhagen, did the Swedes force Denmark to give up the historic provinces of Skåne, Halland, Blekinge and Bohuslän.

Many of the people of Halland, with strong Danish ties, still regard Copenhagen as their logical capital and are less ready than other Swedes to accept the dictates of the central government in Stockholm.

Malmö, the third largest city of Sweden, with a population of more than 235,000, faces Copenhagen across the "Oresund" (the Sound), connecting the Kattegat to the Baltic Sea. Now an important port, Malmö, while actually meaning "sandy island" is legendarily named after a miller's daughter who refused a king. In revenge, he had her ground between two millstones (*mäl-mo*, or "ground maiden").

Just as Götenborg remembers Gustavus Adolphus, Malmö has in its central square a fine statue of Charles X, who brought Malmö into Swedish control in 1658.

Ten miles inland is Lund, the archiepiscopal see for all Scandinavia before 1536. King Canute, the Danish king of England, founded the city and called it Londinium Gothorum, to distinguish it from Londinium, the Roman name of the capital of England. The University of Lund has been famous for hundreds of years, and Lund is also an important publishing city.

Kalmar, the magnificent Renaissance castle on the coast of Småland facing the island of Öland, has been called the "lock and key" of Sweden, and it once dominated all the Baltic shipping.

Here at Kalmar the Union was signed in 1397, an attempt to unite all Scandinavia under one ruler. However, after an uneasy period of civil wars, Kalmar fell to the Danes. In 1638, the *Kalmar Nyckel*, a three-masted sailing ship, sailed from Kalmar to North America with settlers who established a colony on the Delaware River.

The Island of Öland is famous for its wind-

Kalmar is a name that rings through Scandinavian history. It was at 12th-century Kalmar Castle that the Kalmar Union was effected in 1397, combining the crowns of Denmark, Sweden and Norway. Sweden left the Union in 1523, and in the 16th and 17th centuries there were numerous sieges by the Danes during their wars with Sweden. The city of Kalmar was destroyed several times, but the castle withstood all attacks.

mills, its rune stones and for the number of its inhabitants who emigrated to the United States during Sweden's "America fever," most of whom, however, returned to Öland. Here, legend has it, the hero Beowulf is buried. The legend of Beowulf was immortalized in the epic written in Old English before A.D. 1000.

In our journeying across Sweden we must use one or two unusual words—*skerries*, the little rock islands scattered along the coast; *fjells* or fells, bare hills; and *bruk*, a small clearing in the woods where some local industry is going on. At Orrefors, an old bottle-works in a clearing in the forest became within a few years one of the greatest names in glass. Through brilliant designers like Simon Gate and Edvard Hald, Orrefors glass is known all over the world.

NORRLAND

The northern highlands, ranging from central Sweden up through the Arctic Circle, are where the real wealth of the country lies—wood, ore, white coal (sawn timber), iron mines and fast flowing water. It is surprising, therefore, that Norrland supports only 17 per cent of the population. The old peasant culture of the river valleys and the coastal regions, deeply rooted in the Middle Ages, survives here together with the older civilization of the nomadic Lapps. In much of Norrland, the sun never sets during the summer.

North of Dalarna are densely wooded areas, and along the coast of the Gulf of Bothnia are several ports, the major cities of northern Sweden. Gävle, at the southern edge of Norr-

Prince Eugen, brother of the late King Gustavus V, was an outstanding painter and collector. Walde-marsudde, his home on one of Stockholm's islands, became a picture gallery and public garden after his death.

26

Gränna, a small town on the eastern shores of Lake Vättern in Götaland, is set in the heart of some of Sweden's loveliest country.

land, is the oldest and largest city in the upper two-thirds of Sweden. Sundsvall is an important port, while Härnösand and Ümeå are cultural hubs of Norrland. The farther north the port is, the longer it is icebound each year, but Luleå, far into the north, manages to remain an important ore-shipping port.

In every northern river the felled trees lie as plentiful as matchsticks, awaiting the spring thaw to take them miles down to the coastal sawmills. The pounding white water drives the turbines to create electricity, but among the greatest riches of Lapland are the huge iron mountains of Kiruna.

Kiruna, a Lapp word meaning "mountain grouse," is a town of 30,000 inhabitants. The two mountains Kiirunavaara (grouse mountain) and Luossavaara (salmon mountain) produce over 15,000,000 tons of iron ore annually.

While the term "Lapland" refers to a vast territory inhabited by the Lapps that includes parts of Norway, Finland and Russia, the heart of Lapland is in Sweden. The reindeer have long been domesticated and the nomadic Lapps accompany them on their annual migrations between summer grazing on the fjells and winter encampments in the woods.

Surprisingly, the tiny mosquito is the Lapps' best friend. When the reindeer fawns are born in mid-May, the parent reindeer, after eating lichen throughout the long northern winter, are in need of good grass. After three weeks, when the fawn can walk, the summer hatching of mosquitoes drives the herds from the forests in search of the alpine grass their bodies need.

Karesuando, the most northerly Swedish Lapp settlement, consists of a scattered community of wooden dwellings, a Lapp church and a store.

The Östermalm Hall is one of Stockholm's indoor markets. Sweden is largely self-sufficient agriculturally, but many fruits, vegetables and other delicacies are imported.

Örebro Castle, built on an island in the River Svartån in the heart of the Lake District, is used by the governor of the province. Its library is famous for Count Mörner's collections of rare manuscripts, particularly some letters written to the writer August Strindberg by the German philosopher Friedrich Nietzsche when he was going mad. Nietzsche then sometimes signed his letters as "The Crucified."

The Arctic Circle in Sweden is actually marked with white stones! The Gulf Stream gives the area a relatively mild climate during the short summer, despite its latitude.

The "Argentina" forces her way out of the icy port of Göteborg. The Gulf Stream warms Sweden's western coast and allows year-round navigation. The chief steamship company, the Swedish American Line, plies the ocean between New York and Göteborg.

FLORA AND FAUNA

The varying topography and climate in Sweden give rise to many vegetation differences. In the high, mostly northerly alpine region, dwarf shrubs predominate, along with rare occurrences of Arctic poppy. Thick carpets of mosses and lichens share the highest areas with open soil.

Below the alpine belt lie great stands of birch trees which shelter goldenrod and many herbs at their feet. Vast forests of Scotch pine and spruce cover most of the countryside northeast of Lake Vänern. The extensively cultivated land of Skåne supports, for the most part, beech and oak. An old law in Sweden gives everyone access to any forest where 100 types of mushroom can be picked.

Sweden's animal life also shows the effects of the great range of latitude and altitude. Fox, elk, ermine and weasels are found almost everywhere, but the bear, wolf, wolverine and lynx are limited to the deep northern woods and the arctic fox and lemming to the high mountain regions.

The bird community is vast, with the teal, snipe and golden plover the most widespread. The ptarmigan occupies the mountains of the north, along with ducks in the many lakes found there. Elsewhere, grouse, cranes, partridge and an occasional sea eagle are found.

The rivers, lakes, and estuaries abound with salmon, trout, pike, herring, cod and mackerel.

Pine, spruce, birch and fir—Sweden is like an ocean of waving trees. These giants are stock trees in a replanted forest.

To the north of Sweden the land rises. This is an upland pasture in Medelpad, an historic province which is now administratively part of the province of Västernorrland.

The Three Crowns Flour Mill works far into the night. Modern factories and greater automation help keep Sweden's industries flourishing.

3. ECONOMY

TODAY, Sweden is a great economic power, and its people have the highest standard of living in Europe. Agriculture has been replaced by industry as the mainstay of Sweden's economy. Since 1900, the industrial capacity of Sweden has multiplied by more than five times, and now only 8 per cent of the workers are still employed in agriculture.

Although 90 per cent of the work force are employed by private companies, Sweden's government participates in many economic activities, as do the co-operatives, which are operated mainly by consumers in the retailing field and by farmers in marketing and purchasing. The state is most active in service indus-

tries, such as rail and bus lines, power, the post office, telephones, radio and television (the latter owned by a subsidiary company of the State alcohol monopoly). The extensive state-owned forests own factories for the manufacture of wooden houses and other wooden goods, competing with privately owned firms. Most state-owned enterprises are *aktiebolag* (joint stock corporations) and are subject to the Swedish Corporations Act. Often having a proportion of private stockholders, they enjoy no privileges over private corporations.

The state has a half-share in SAS, the joint Swedish-Danish-Norwegian airline, and 42 per cent of the electric power in the country is

The glass industry is still dependent upon the skills of individual artisans. Here a master craftsman examines his almost finished crystal bowl.

AGRICULTURE

Only 10 per cent of Sweden's land is arable (compared to 30 per cent in Britain, and 60 per cent in Denmark) and supporting the entire population was for many years a major problem. However, with hard work, expert soil study, upgrading of fertilizers and breeding, crop rotation and mechanization, the problem has been successfully met. Every year more and more people leave the farms for the cities, but every year the yield from agriculture goes up. It is truly remarkable that Sweden has remained self-sufficient agriculturally.

FORESTS AND FOREST PRODUCTS

Three factors are responsible for the healthy state of Sweden's forest industries: rich pine and fir stands; the rivers flowing southeastward down the mountains, which in the past provided cheap transportation for the timber although today most of the logs are hauled by road; and, very important also, excellent conservation measures, such as selective cutting

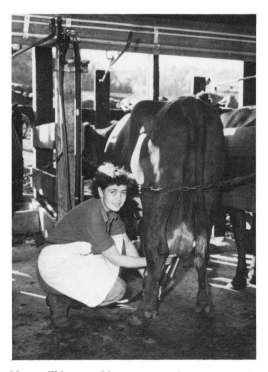

produced in state plants. The state also owns all the ore deposits in Upper Norrland in the north of the country. Yet free enterprise is maintained as the basis of the system, and relatively few industries have been nationalized.

Iron, wood and water—out of these three resources the Swedes have created their economy. The rich copper mine at Falun which brought the Swedes such wealth is worked out, but the huge new mines discovered in Lapland have replaced it. Even more important and forever being replenished are the forests that cover more than half the country and provide many of Sweden's exports—timber, pulp and paper. The rivers, cascading through the forests, provide electric power for the nation's industries.

Exports are very important, for the money earned from these allows Sweden to import the materials it needs for industry and private use. The traditional liberal trading regulations and low tariffs have helped foreign trade prosper.

New milking machines are tested at an experimental farm.

The forests are Sweden's wealth. The logs are brought to the processing mills by both river and road.

and systematic replanting, which have allowed logging to increase without depleting the forests severely.

In addition to the large lumber industry, the wood is also used to make pulp and paper. Several inventions by Swedish engineers, now spread round the world, helped Sweden establish its importance in these fields many years ago. Especially important is cellulose, or chemical wood pulp, of which Sweden is a leading producer.

Once responsible for one-third of the world's iron output, Sweden was hurt by the discovery of coal as a smelting agent. Yet it has fought to

Heavy-duty tractors are used to haul sawn timber from the forest.

An aluminium ingot is re-melted at the Finspong Metal Works. The furnaces there can melt up to 100 tons per day.

←

maintain its importance as a steel producer by turning to high quality steel and exporting the iron ore to other ore-poor countries. The steel is used by Sweden in many of its industries, such as in the manufacture of ball bearings, razor blades and saws. In addition to iron ore, zinc as well as lead and copper are mined in Sweden.

SHIPBUILDING

Sweden has expanded its shipbuilding so much since World War II that it usually ranks among the top three building nations each year, although the industry receives no government subsidy. The majority of the ships are sold to Norway, other major customers being the USSR and Great Britain.

The old economy and the new—the water-power station on the Indalsälven, one of the great power-producing rivers of Sweden. In the foreground a farmer rakes his hay with one horse-power.

Göteborg's economy is largely dependent on the sea. Shipbuilding has been an industry of the city for hundreds of years, and new boats are built for many different countries.

Swedish logs are being sent to factories producing timber for houses and other wood products as well as pulp for paper mills. Man-made timber chutes facilitate moving the logs from the forests to the rivers.

CHEMICALS

Although it lacks many of the raw materials needed for large-scale chemical industries, Sweden has long been dominant in the match and explosive fields. J. E. Lundström invented the safety match in the 19th century and gave his country the lead in production. With the

The Swedish Primus stove is exported throughout the world. It is so popular that many people refer to every kerosene (paraffin) stove as a "primus." They are polished by hand in the factory before being shipped out.

A great platter is turned at the famous Orrefors Glassworks.

Sven Wingquist, founder of SKF, the Swedish Ball Bearing Co., revolutionized the ball bearing industry with his invention of self-aligning ball bearings. Here they are being assembled at the SKF factory.

Silver from the sea—a rich haul of herring on the coast off Bohuslän will be rushed to the fish market.

On Sweden's Baltic coast, a fisherman's wife on the Isle of Ulvön sits on the wharf mending her husband's nets.

collapse of the Ivar Kreuger match trust, an international match monopoly, in the 1930's, match production did decline somewhat, but myriads of the felled trees still reach Jönköping on Lake Vättern to be chopped into matchsticks by the Swedish Match Company.

Alfred B. Nobel, founder of the Nobel Prizes, invented dynamite in 1866 and laid the foundation of the dynamite industry. While explosive manufacture is still important in Sweden, almost the total output is exported.

A sizeable industry has developed to make use of the by-products of chemical wood pulping. Further processing yields celluloid, lacquer, glue, turpentine, resins, and other materials.

ENGINEERING

The output of cars, trucks, buses, electrical machinery, ball bearings, razor blades, and other engineering products has grown tremendously in Sweden. In fact the engineering industries employ five times as many people as the next largest industry and produce the greatest volume of exports.

TEXTILES

Sweden is not only a major producer of textiles, an industry which employs over 90,000 people, but is also a major consumer of them. As a matter of fact, the average Swede consumes more textiles than citizens of any other country except the United States and Canada.

FOREIGN TRADE

Foreign trade is very important to Sweden's economy. The many exports do not quite balance the imports, the most important of which are mineral oils, coal and coke, and finished iron and steel. The exports are mainly timber, pulp, paper and board, iron ore, finished iron and steel, and engineering products and machinery.

Since 1964, Sweden has tripled its foreign trade. The two chief trading partners are West Germany and Great Britain. Sweden is a member of EFTA, the European Free Trade Association, and GATT, the General Agreement on Trade and Tariffs. It also trades extensively with countries of the European Common Market.

This cable conveyor, built by the Nordström Company, linking the mines at Kristineberg with the works at Boliden in northern Sweden, may be the longest in the world. Its capacity is 50 tons per hour.

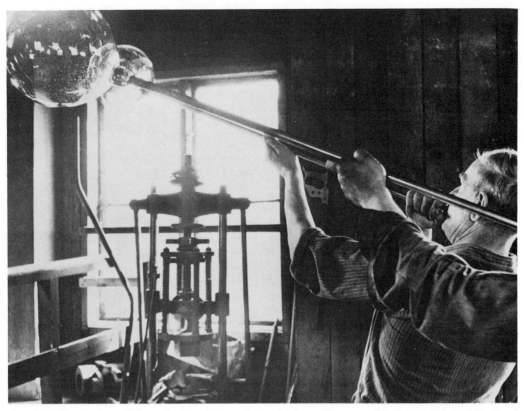

Orrefors Glassworks, which sends glass all over the world, is an almost rural industry set in the Småland forests. Some 40 glassworks are found within a radius of 30 miles in the area, which supplies them with ample water and fuel for power. Blowing the glass, shown here, is an important step in the manufacturing process.

Engraving is accomplished by holding the glass to the emery wheel.

Fiddlers play and the country folk dance in the traditional costume of 1850 Värmland.

4. PEOPLE

THERE ARE IN SWEDEN about 8,200,000 people, equal to the population of either London or New York, but less than that of Denmark and Norway combined.

A joke about Swedish formality and love of titles is that told of two passengers on a ship, who wishing to speak, but finding no way of knowing each other's status, hit on the idea of addressing each other as "Mr. Steamship Passenger." This is one side of the picture. The other is of a well-balanced people, reserved yet passionate, a tall, sombre, good-looking people with innate good taste that is reflected in their architecture, their design and, above all, in their way of living.

Another insight into the Swedish character is gained by contrasting them with their fellow Scandinavians. The Danes call themselves the French of the Baltic; the Norwegians are wilder and happy-go-lucky; the Finns, from their long struggle for statehood, are stubborn and individualistic; while the Swedes, with Germanic efficiency and orderliness, are really full of enthusiasm once their reserve is pierced. The northern Swedes, however, still-faced and slant-eyed, have something of Mongolian impassivity.

Perhaps the greatest single talent of the Swedes is for organization, for managing to run things as frictionlessly, efficiently and practically as possible despite every difficulty. For instance, in spite of the enormously high wages and taxes industrialists must pay, Sweden can still export successfully and even compete successfully, as they do with the Japanese in shipbuilding. Setbacks and obstacles are immediately met with rationalization.

There are disadvantages to the Swedish passion for orderliness, however. The most characteristic of all Swedish words is said to be *kontrollstyrelse*, which means controlling authority, and the best illustration of this is the enormously elaborate structure of the government, with its ministries, governmental institutes, state departments, commissions, committees, secretariats, inspectorates, and so on. These account in large measure for the heavy burden of the taxpayer. If our two steamship passengers mentioned above found themselves shipwrecked on a desert island, it is highly likely they would immediately set up a kontrollstyrelse in order to rationalize their life together.

EDUCATION

Sweden has almost no illiteracy—nearly every person can read and write. Responsible for this wonderful record are the compulsory education laws and the great value the Swedish people themselves place on education.

Since 1842, every Swedish child has had to go to school for at least 7 years. Recently, the State School system has introduced the 9-year compulsory school all over the country, aiming to give every child a chance to obtain a higher as well as a primary education. The Ministry of Education has also been moving to make the local provinces responsible for the schools, with the State inspectors as servants, rather than directors, of the schools.

The compulsory 9-year schools take pupils from 7 to 16, while the upper secondary schools, called *gymnasiums*, allow about 25 per cent of the students (at present) to continue their education another three years. It is expected that by 1970 the proportion will rise to at least 30 per cent, and that at least a further 20 per cent will attend continuation schools (*fackskolor*) for two years' general theoretical instruction in semi-industrial or vocational training schools, or full-time courses at vocational schools (*yrkes-skolor*).

These wee folk are not the "little people" the Laplanders say they sometimes see, but pupils at a nursery school.

Free school meals are common in Sweden. One little girl is going back to the serving table, like Oliver Twist, to ask for more. Milk is drunk out of tetrahedral (four-sided) cartons.

At present there is a reform in progress converting the 9-year compulsory school into a co-educational "comprehensive school" (*enhetsskola*) which will replace the primary schools, the lower secondary schools (*realskolor*) and schools for girls only. The system is similar to that in England, and there is no leaving-examination upon completion.

Some students who have finished at the *gymnasium* go on to one of the five universities in Sweden: Uppsala, Lund, Stockholm, Göteborg and, in the north, Ümeå. Within these are 20 colleges or professional schools.

In addition to the state schools, there are 25-state-aided private schools and 100 Folk High Schools, a typically Scandinavian phenomenon, with the minimum entry age of 18. These Folk High Schools have played an important part in Swedish life along with the free and voluntary educational movement. All

tuition is free, all textbooks are free and almost all schools provide one cooked meal a day.

Vocational schools such as those mentioned above, often supported by the state, counties and municipalities, are active in giving vocational training in trade, agriculture, forestry, nursing, etc. And, in addition to formal education, Sweden has a widespread adult education scheme, and many correspondence schools are popular with students in remote areas.

SOCIAL WELFARE POLICY

Many factors have led Sweden to become advanced in its social welfare facilities. For centuries the concept of mutual help has been present in the country. This, with the rapid growth and the impact of industrialization, led to welfare schemes in the 19th century, and in

Students serenade beneath a girl's window in the old university town of Uppsala. But she doesn't seem to be home!

One of Stockholm's fine new hospitals, Nacka Lasarett. Under Sweden's social welfare policies, all patients receive free medical care and free medicine for chronic illnesses. The social services require one-third of Sweden's budget.

the 20th century these schemes have undergone spectacular expansion.

Socialized medicine and the other social welfare reforms had roots in the rapid rise from a poor agricultural economy to a flourish- ing industrial economy, with a large class of workers who had had personal experience of poverty, unemployment and insecurity. They joined the Social Democratic Party, which has been in power for three decades and pursues a

Modern libraries help make books available to the Swedish people, most of whom are avid readers.

conservative fiscal policy. The party led a battery of social reforms covering health, unemployment, old-age, workmen's compensation, child care, etc. The last major reform occurred in 1959 when a national supplementary pensions plan was adopted by a one-vote majority, largely through the efforts of Tage Erlander, the prime minister. This new pensions scheme will eventually guarantee everyone a retirement pension amounting to about 60 per cent of the average income earned in the most prosperous 15 years of his or her working life.

Taxes, particularly the sales tax, are admittedly quite high, and there is an increasing trend towards the feeling that direct taxation rather than the present indirect taxation would be a greater advantage for the poor. But one-third of the total government budget is spent on social welfare (far more than on defence) and the Swedish people seem content with the security, health, and happiness which the welfare policies induce, so that there is no serious challenge to either high taxation or government policies.

OLD-AGE PENSIONS

Every citizen who has reached his 67th year receives a basic old-age pension, plus a cost-of-living bonus, and a supplementary amount financed by himself and/or by his former employers. The retired Swede thus draws almost two-thirds of his normal income, but the rather heavy income taxes apply to this money. Every citizen between 16 and 66 who is not an employed wage-earner makes a regular contribution to this pension plan, and the remainder of the money comes from employers and the regular government budget.

The Stadshuset, or City Hall, is a well-known building on the shore of Lake Mälaren in Stockholm. One of the chief landmarks of the city, it was designed by Ragnar Östberg and opened in 1923.

45

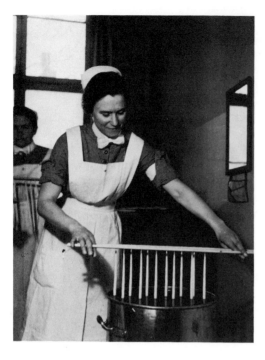

Candle-making for Christmas is not a job but a joy for this nurse. Repeated dipping of the wicks in tallow-grease gives the candles their shape. Candles in Sweden are the best way of lighting up Christmas, which falls close to the dark days of ← the winter solstice.

COMPULSORY HEALTH INSURANCE

Since 1955, every citizen has been covered by compulsory health insurance which provides compensation for income lost due to accident or illness and takes care of the total cost of hospital treatment, a large share of the cost of medicine and doctors' bills, and travel expense incurred in serious illness and hospitalization.

UNEMPLOYMENT INSURANCE

The government helps support the unemployment insurance funds of the trade unions and similar organizations, and pays directly the very few unemployed who are not in these groups.

MATERNITY BENEFITS

All pregnant mothers receive free prenatal care, free hospital service at delivery, and cash allowances for some time after delivery. There are special supplements to help needy mothers provide adequately for their children. Largely as a result of this scheme, nearly every child is born in a hospital and the infant mortality rate is among the lowest in the world.

WORKMEN'S COMPENSATION

Every employee in Sweden knows that if he is injured on the job or off, he will receive enough money to preserve the living standard of himself and his family.

CHILD CARE

Sweden feels that its children are especially important and must be taken care of as adequately as possible. Some of the governmental services for their benefit are free medical checkups; free dental care; free school lunches in most schools; scholarships to allow higher education; vocational training for poor children; housing subsidies to the parents so they can provide adequate housing for their family; free vacation travel money for children and

Emanuel Swedenborg, one of the great 18th-century intellects, was an engineer, scientist, physicist, geologist, physiologist, philosopher and mystic. Unintentionally, he started a new religious movement which still has adherents, mainly in the United States and England. →

further severity is imposed. Open prisons, devoid of forbidding bars and resembling large farms, have replaced the old barred institutions to a great extent.

Sweden does not believe in breaking a prisoner's spirit, and a man may, through the work of his hands, make some restitution to whomever he has injured.

RELIGION AND FESTIVALS

Sweden, like the other Scandinavian countries, is overwhelmingly Protestant. The state church, the Church of Sweden, is Evangelical Lutheran. Over 90 per cent of the Swedes are baptized and married by the Church of Sweden, and there are only about 600,000 nonconformists to the prevailing religion—mostly in other branches of Protestantism.

their mother; subsidies for day nurseries and summer camps; and an additional allowance to all mothers for each child under 16. In addition to this government aid, many institutions and industrial corporations provide extensive social benefits for their employees.

PENAL LAWS

On July 1, 1946, a new law went into effect providing that prisoners should always be treated with regard to their dignity as human beings. There has been no execution since 1910 and in 1921 the death penalty was abolished. While half the male prisoners are sentenced to hard work (usually lumbering in the north) no

The Nobel Medals are awarded for eminence in physics, chemistry, physiology and medicine, and literature. The peace prize, when it is warranted, is also awarded. Alfred Nobel, inventor of dynamite, left a fund to provide the prizes named after him. ⟶

Going to church in the lake country of Dalarna often meant going by boat in old times, but now cycles and buses are preferred. On Midsummer Day, however, the old church-boats still put out with the villagers dressed in their finery.

Several of Sweden's biggest festivals are religious in origin. The most elaborate festival is Christmas, which lasts from Christmas Eve to Twelfth Night or even to St. Knut's Day on January 14. On New Year's Eve, the Swedes try to read their fortunes by interpreting the figures produced by molten lead poured into cold water. On New Year's Day everyone visits, and traditionally the governors, bishops and senior officials receive visits from their subordinates.

Lady Day, March 25, is devoted to the Virgin Mary. It falls near the spring equinox, when the day is as long as the night.

Easter brings out small girls with blackened faces astride broomsticks. This phenomenon results from the belief that the witches flew off on Maundy Thursday to confer with the Evil One.

Walpurgis Eve comes on April 30 with bonfire celebrations and a eulogy on the advent of spring, the spirit of the fire marking the sun's return. Walpurgis has survived from Viking times when the warriors held an annual feast to herald the return of spring, lighting bonfires on the hills and banging their sword hilts against their shields to frighten off evil spirits.

All Sweden awaits Midsummer Day with its tall, leaf-decked Maypoles, when everything is decorated with flowers and birch twigs. It is on Midsummer Eve that girls place seven different flowers under their pillows to dream of the man they will marry, hoping that on Midsummer Day, when all the costumes are put on for dancing round the Maypole, they will meet him in the *ringdans* (ring dance) or perhaps in the *långdans* (long dance). It was on Midsummer Day in 1523 that Gustavus Vasa liberated Sweden and entered Stockholm at the head of his troops.

On Walpurgis Eve (April 30) thousands of Uppsala's university students in their white caps salute the sun's return behind the spires of the cathedral.

August Strindberg wrote 70 plays. Among the best known are "The Father" (1887) and "Miss Julie" (1888). Brilliant, violent and controversial, Strindberg always attacked smug conventionality. Much of his fiction concerns his three unhappy marriages.

LITERATURE

Swedish literature may still be best known to many people for its sagas, Eddas, and ballads which were rooted in the old Norse myths. These writings were important expressions of Scandinavian ethics and mythology, but Swedish literature has by no means been stagnant since the Middle Ages.

During the 17th century, Sweden was a major power in Europe and played an active part in Renaissance culture. Georg Stiernhielm, called the Father of Swedish Poetry, set out to show that the Swedish language could be used in the classic metres of poetry. Poetry was the strength of Sweden's literature for a long period after Stiernhielm.

Gustavus III, with his Swedish Academy, Dramatic Theatre and Royal Opera, was the leading light in the expansion of 18th-century culture, which was derived largely from imitation of the French.

In the 19th century, literary taste was influenced by Germany. This romantic era was perhaps the greatest in Swedish literature. In one school were the pure romanticists such as Per Daniel Amadeus Atterbom, a poet, mystic and dreamer, and Erik Johan Stagnelius, who also expressed a yearning for a world of fantasy. The Gothic Society, on the other hand, included a group of men who were interested in the past, in the old traditions which they considered glorious. Erik Gustaf Geijer, philosopher, historian, poet and musician, and Esaias Tegnér, the brilliant exponent of the classic tradition and champion of Platonic idealism, were both members of the Society, founded in 1811.

The middle of the 19th century saw Swedish literature sway between realism and idealism. The first modern newspaper, *Aftonbladet*, was founded in 1830, and Carl Jonas Love Almqvist,

Greta Garbo ranks as one of the great screen personalities of all time. She attended the Royal Dramatic Academy in Stockholm, the city of her birth, and her success in a Swedish film brought her to the attention of Hollywood.

Sweden has had many actresses who have become internationally famous. Viveca Lindfors is known for her starring rôles in theatre productions and films. Here she appears in "The Serious Jest" by the Swedish dramatist Hjalmar Söderberg.

with exotic adventure stories and sensitive folk tales, became one of the most gifted writers of the times.

Modern Swedish literature began with, and is still strongly under the influence of, August Strindberg. He was the first to write realistic social interpretation, and his experimental poetry and expressionistic dramas are still studied and imitated. He was bitingly satirical of bureaucracy, bourgeois life and marriage, and his "superman" philosophy, his woman-hating and his terrible bitterness made him both controversial and despised.

Selma Lagerlöf (1858–1940) wrote novels and tales dealing with the peasant life of her native district of Varmland, a region rich in folklore and rustic tradition. Her children's book, "The Wonderful Adventures of Nils," has become a classic, while her celebrated novel, "Gösta Berling" was made into a film whose success raised Greta Garbo, its star, to the top rank of the film industry. Selma Lagerlöf is also remembered as the first Swede to win a Nobel Prize.

Ingmar Bergman, who has directed, written and produced many cinema films, is best known for his "The Seventh Seal," "Wild Strawberries," and "Virgin Spring."

Alf Sjöberg served as First Director at the Royal Dramatic Theatre in Stockholm.

Carl von Linné, who Latinized his name to Carolus Linnaeus, originated scientific classification of plants and animals, and he named and described over 10,000 species of plants. He lived at Uppsala, where he was buried in 1778. His title is justly royal: "The King of Flowers."

Alfred Bernhard Nobel is doubly famous. First he invented dynamite in 1866. Second, as a result of his pacifist philosophy, he left a fund to provide the Nobel Prizes. The small Nobel factory where his family worked on explosives was in Heleneborg.

The literature of the 20th century has been mainly in a realistic vein. Novelists, short-story writers and playwrights have become more important than poets. The traditional ideals and values have been shattered, and experimentation in literary forms has continued to be very important. Swedish prose was given a lift by Hjalmar Bergman, and Pär Lagerkvist has dominated much of the rebellious, critical writing of this century.

Strindberg's play "Ett Drömspel"—"A Dream Play"—was recently produced in Stockholm.

Dag Hammarskjöld, the late Secretary-General of the United Nations, had bought a farm in Skåne to which he planned to retire, but he never reached it. The plane that was taking him to the Congo crashed and he was killed on Sept. 18, 1961.

U Thant paid respects at the grave of Dag Hammarskjöld in Uppsala, the town where the late Secretary-General of the United Nations was educated. The son of a prominent political family, Hammarskjöld entered government service in 1930. As Secretary-General from 1953–1961, he performed a service to the entire world, and he was awarded the Nobel Peace Prize posthumously in 1961.

53

The Water Lily House is typical of the stimulating architectural designs of modern Sweden. The roof of this house opens to sunlight like the petals of a water lily, but closes by the mere push of a button.

ARTS AND CRAFTS

For a thousand years, Swedish objects have been studied for their artistic values, but it has been in this century that Sweden has enjoyed its greatest influence on arts and crafts.

The beautiful old stone churches dating from before the Middle Ages were not just imitations of architecture in other countries; rather, prototypes were adapted to the Swedish landscape. The castles of the 16th century show the same adaptation, and, remarkably, even modern Swedish architecture, characterized by its simplicity and functional nature, is strongly suited to its Swedish setting. The Swedes think that design in buildings is important, and even the massive new apartment buildings and factories are often architectural gems.

Swedish sculpture has in recent years been identified with Carl Milles, but the wood and stone carvers on Gotland in the Middle Ages were famous. The old churches of Gotland and the mainland of Sweden are still filled with the beautiful fonts, screens and images by these artists.

The Swedes apply the most lofty principles of beauty and design to even the simplest utensils and furnishings of daily life. With the innate Swedish love of things artistic, it is not surprising to find their greatest strength is in design. Sweden, an isolated and old agricultural country suddenly turned modern in a wave of rapid industrialization, has based clean new lines on the severe foundations of older traditions.

Isolation forced Sweden to develop its own resources (ironmaking, for example, goes back 2000 years) and from this springs the versatile uses of steel, wood, clay and glass. It must be remembered, too, that since Viking times sailors, tradesmen and merchants have brought

Life class at a Stockholm art school brings great concentration from budding artists. This girl is modelling in clay.

Count Sigvard Bernadotte, of the royal family of Sweden, as a famous designer with Georg Jensen, has given much thought to making ordinary household objects more beautiful. ⟶

The potter at work on a vase.

Skörstorp is the only remaining round church left in Västergötland. The separate bell tower can be seen on the left.

Authentic Swedish rugs are still woven with the aid of simple looms.

At the Orrefors Glass Works, many artists produce masterpieces, such as this bottle and glass designed by Hald.

ally tried in Great Britain, while shopping centres arose in the United States in response to the acute problems arising from the growing use of private cars. Sweden, also faced with a relatively large number of private cars, found it best to apply town planning ideas to shopping centres and to make them real meeting places for the whole community. The most modern centres comprise not only department stores, supermarkets, and abundant smaller special shops but also public buildings, banks, libraries, theatres and cinemas, medical clinics and "doctors' houses"—where the town's specialists, dentists and general practitioners are all to be found under one roof—and post offices, kindergartens etc. Cars are banned within the centre, all its highways being for pedestrians only.

back goods and ideas to Sweden from all over the world.

Swedish society seldom gave room for feudal grandeur. The granite churches, the manor houses and the farms all have the mark of simplicity, almost of austerity. French influence during the 18th century helped to mellow this, and native art, together with the impulses of rising commerce and industry, have produced "Modern Swedish" design—in glass, ceramics, textiles, furniture, silver and stainless steel.

SHOPPING CENTRES

In connection with Sweden's town and country planning, the new suburban shopping centres have attracted much notice in other countries. Town planning schemes were origin-

An engraved decanter with stopper by the artist Palmquist.

57

The northern part of Sweden, including much territory within the Arctic Circle, is known as Lapland. The native Lapps are greatly outnumbered by descendants of settlers of the past few hundred years. Here a Lapp lady, on one knee, is milking a doe. Notice the spreading hoofs which prevent the reindeer from sinking through the snow.

LAPLANDERS

The origin of the Lapps, living in the far north of Scandinavia, is still something of a mystery but they are generally believed to have come from central Asia. Although they speak a form of the Finnish language, they are not Finns. They appear to be the first race to have inhabited Norrland. Thirty-four thousand Laplanders, all told, live in Sweden, Norway, Finland and the Kola Peninsula of Russia. Sweden has about 10,000 of them, many of whom are nomads tending their reindeer herds.

While Sweden educates the young Lapp children in nomad schools which follow the herds, the older children must attend "anchored" schools in the forest.

Laplanders are allowed all the reindeer they wish, although a Swede may have no more than 20 in a herd, for the reindeer is the very life-blood of the Lapps. Besides being a very handsome animal, both male and female having large antlers, the reindeer is a draught animal. The flesh provides venison; the doe gives milk which can be made into cheese, the bones make implements; and the skins make warm clothing and tents.

Their skin tents are easily movable and hauled on the boat-like sled (*gieres*) behind their reindeer. Other equipment is the pack-frame (*spagat*), the ski and the lasso. Archaeological finds have established that the Lapps used the ski as far back as the Stone Age. The lasso is also used by the Russian Samoyeds and the American Indians.

The Lapps, nominally Christian, brightly clad in their scarlet, yellow and blue dress, sometimes take their dogs with them into church. "Why shouldn't they come in to talk to God, too?" they ask.

While the Lapps have no written literature to speak of, their oral literature is very rich. One type of song is *yoiking*, a rhythmical song-poem. A winter love song goes like this:

"Kulnasatj, my little reindeer,
it is time for us to journey,
set off to the northern forest,
hasten over spreading swampland,
journey to the fair one's home.
Run more swiftly now, my reindeer,
so that we may come the sooner
to the one that Sarak sent me,
to the one that is my fate.
Ah, if soon I might behold her,
rest my eyes on my beloved!
Kulnasatj, my little reindeer,
Can you not now see her eyes?"

The metre used in this poem is the Finnish "trochaic" which was borrowed by Longfellow for his *The Song of Hiawatha*.

RECREATION

The Swedes are enthusiastic about out-of-doors activities. Many go to country homes or sports cabins out in the country whenever they get a chance, and nearly everyone rides bicycles or takes motor trips during the summer. As in many European countries, soccer is the most popular sport. Skiing is both a recreation and a necessity in Sweden: many times skis are used when the other means of transportation are paralyzed by snow and ice. Tennis, golf, ice hockey and track and field athletics are other sports which the Swedes find time for.

Swedish gymnastics, popular in much of the world, are still a required part of the school curriculum. Many adults never get out of the practice of doing these exercises even after they finish school.

On a March day every year, thousands of cross-country skiers speed over 54 miles of Swedish country-side in the "Vasaloppet," the Vasa Ski Race, to commemorate a trip taken by Gustavus Vasa in 1523. Escaping from the Danes, Gustavus appealed to the Dalecarlians for support. When they refused, he set off on skis from Mora. Soon after he had left, the Dalecarlians changed their minds about supporting Gustavus and sent out two speedy skiers who overtook him in Sälen, 54 miles from Mora. The commemorative race is now run in the opposite direction, from Sälen to Mora, for technical reasons, but the distance is the same.

Cross-country skiing through the snowy woods in winter takes the place of summer sun-worshipping.

Smörgåsbord (meaning bread-and-butter table) has everything to delight the eye and the palate. Even the polar bear seems ready to eat. "Skål," the Norse toast, actually means "bowl," the vessel from which the fearless Vikings drank. Glögg, a hot Christmas drink, is made from "snaps" and steaming spiced wine.

The Riksdag (Parliament House) is one of the most important buildings in Stockholm. The first Riksdag was organized in 1435 by the nobleman Engelbrekt Engelbrektsson.

5. GOVERNMENT

SWEDEN is a unitary national state and not a federation. At the present time there are 24 districts, plus Stockholm, each with a governor appointed by the central government, but there are plans for a new division into fewer units. The districts still maintain some small degree of self-rule.

Historically, Sweden has been divided into 25 provinces, or *landskap*. The provinces are a result of the loose federation of feudal organizations during the Middle Ages, and many people still think in terms of the historical provinces rather than the administrative districts. These provinces retain distinctive characteristics and are often the units of patriotic sentiment.

GOVERNMENTAL UNITS

The king of Sweden exerts no political power and takes no part in politics. He represents the nation as the Head of State, and in this capacity formerly signed all important decisions of the government. In 1973, however, new constitutional laws stripped the king of all vestiges of power, including the signing of decisions. The real responsibility rests with the prime minister and the cabinet ministers.

If a cabinet resigns for political reasons, it is up to the speaker of Parliament to find a prime minister who can form a new cabinet with the strongest parliamentary support. Although appointed by the speaker, the prime minister's power derives from a majority in the Riksdag. The prime minister is assisted by a cabinet of 15 ministers.

The Riksdag, one of the oldest legislative bodies in the world, formerly consisted of two houses of equal rank. Effective January, 1975, a new constitution established a one-chamber legislature, with 349 members serving 3-year terms.

THE OLD CONSTITUTION

The Swedish Instrument of Government of 1809 was frequently amended; the document still shows traces of the 18th century. Because it reflected a long and varied constitutional development ranging from royal absolutism to curious forms of parliamentary procedure, it has been called "the history of the Swedish people in 114 Articles."

The story behind this constitution is brief

and dramatic. On March 13, 1809, officers arrested the hapless Gustavus IV Adolphus when he had brought Sweden to the verge of catastrophe. The King's uncle, Duke Charles, called the Four Estates to meet in Stockholm. The new Instrument of Government was drafted in less than three weeks (the country being surrounded by enemies—Denmark to the south, and Russia massed on the north), and it was passed by the three Higher Estates—the Nobility, the Clergy and the Burghers. The Fourth Estate, the Peasants, held out for several noble privileges to be revoked before signing. Extreme haste was needed to form some recognizable government merely to sue for peace with the Czar of Russia and the Danish King.

The spade work of this constitution was done by Anders af Håkansson, who was not a revolutionary but a civil servant who had the confidence of the Regent. Most of his proposals were adopted.

THE PARTY SYSTEM

There are now five parties represented in the Swedish Riksdag. The oldest and largest is the Social Democrats, formed in 1889. Abandoning its early Marxian principles, it developed into a moderate reform socialist party. Its local organizations, the workers' communes, are based on both individual membership and block affiliation through trade union membership.

By the time the Liberal Party had formed in 1900, the classic demands of liberal doctrine had to a great extent been realized. The party's present policies have been described as social liberalism, in which many welfare policies are combined with ways of promoting individual initiative and freedom of enterprise. The Liberal Party, although weak in organization, has strong support from the press.

The Centre Party, previously called the Farmers' Party, was formed in 1913. Although comparatively small, it is well organized and plays a decisive rôle in politics. As its old name suggests, it represents the farmers' interests, the majority of its supporters being independent farmers.

King Gustavus VI Adolphus succeeded his father, Gustavus V, in 1950. An enormously popular king, he was a familiar sight in the streets of Stockholm where he walked about freely. An ardent archeologist, he spent considerable time on "digs" round the world. Following his death in 1973, his grandson, Crown Prince Charles Gustavus acceded to the throne as King Charles XVI Gustavus.

In 1904, rural and urban groups established a General Electoral Association. This led to a strong conservative organization now backed by the Conservative Party. While 30 per cent of those who vote Conservative come from the top social levels, most of the support is from the middle classes. With a strong press, the Conservatives maintain a position as an active opposition party.

The Communist Party, formed in 1921, has a membership of only 25,000 and is little more than a mouthpiece for the Moscow-directed international communist movement. Its strongholds are in the far north and in parts of Stockholm and Göteborg.

THE NORDIC COUNCIL

Since it has been an old dream to unite Scandinavia, the initiative was taken in 1951 to establish a Nordic Council. Meeting in Copenhagen in 1953, it formed a joint consultative organ to consider questions, other than defence and security, arising in Denmark, Finland, Iceland, Norway and Sweden.

The Nordic Council has 69 elected members, only five of whom are from Iceland, and acts as a forum of debate. In legal matters the work has been towards common legislation. The Council has helped to lighten customs and passport regulations and has worked in the areas of culture and social welfare.

THE OMBUDSMAN

One of Sweden's government inventions is that of the ombudsman. Established in 1809, the ombudsman is essentially a "watchdog," the representative of an institution for protecting citizens against abuses by government officials. He developed into a means whereby citizens could voice their complaints and get fast action, and this feature has appealed so much to other countries that recently many of them have appointed an ombudsman themselves.

The magnificently gilded Royal Coach, kept in the Royal Palace, carries new ambassadors to present their credentials to the king.

INDEX